Daniel And The Spanish Robot

Daniel Meets The Spanish Robot

One day a Spanish robot came to live with Daniel and his family.

¡Hola!
Me llamo Robot.

¡Hola!
Me llamo Daniel.

Daniel knew that **Hola** meant hello.

He also remembered **Me llamo** meant my name is…. so he introduced himself in Spanish.

They soon became best friends.

All of his friends loved coming round to play. And the Spanish robot loved joining in, well, as long as they spoke in Spanish!

The Spanish robot would always ask Daniel's friends how they were when they arrived. Today both of his friends replied that they were feeling good.

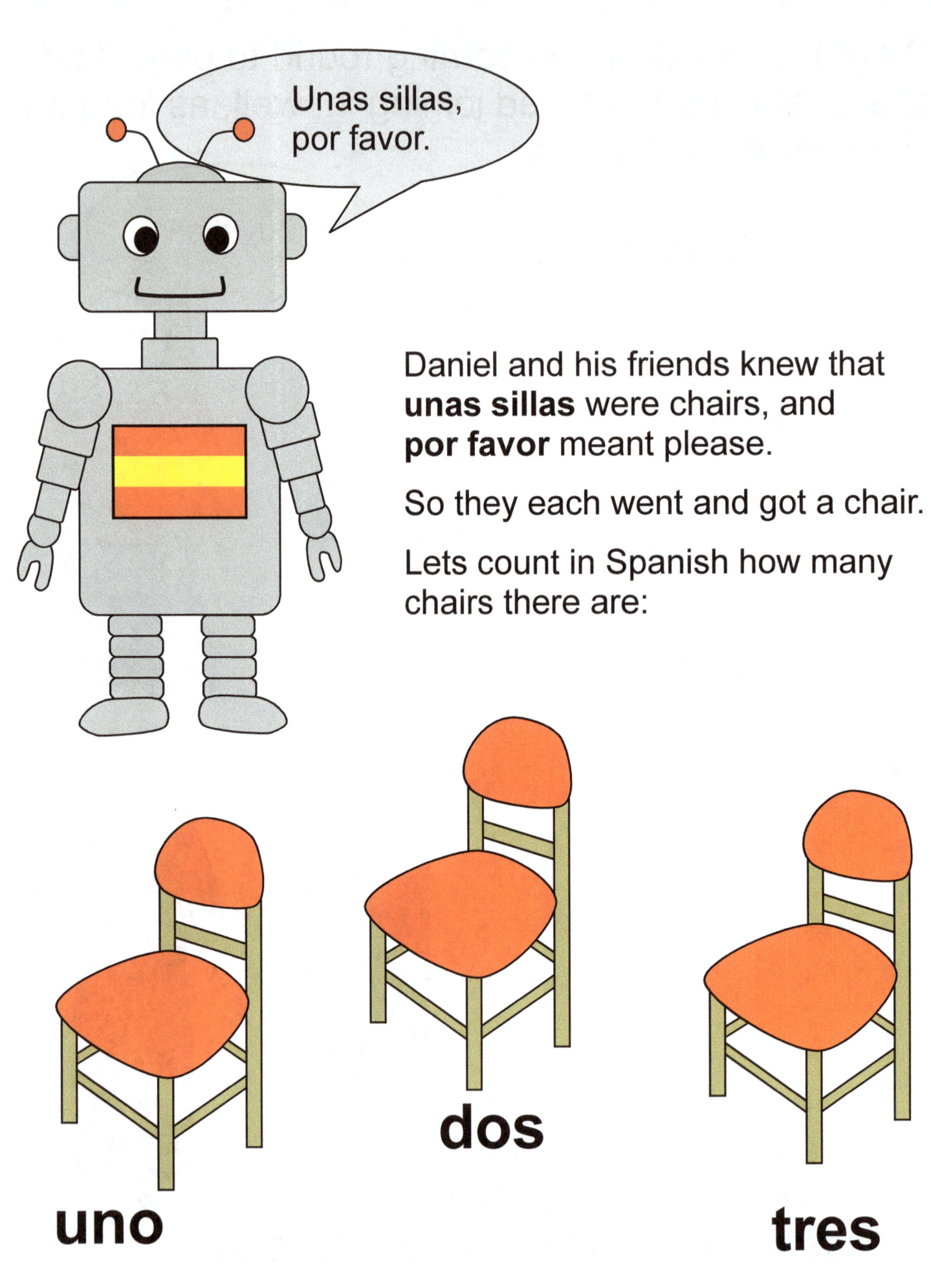

Now the Spanish robot was amazing to play with as he could make images appear, well, as long as **everyone** said three times the Spanish word for the thing they wanted.

Everyone moved their chairs into position, and the robot beamed an image of…..

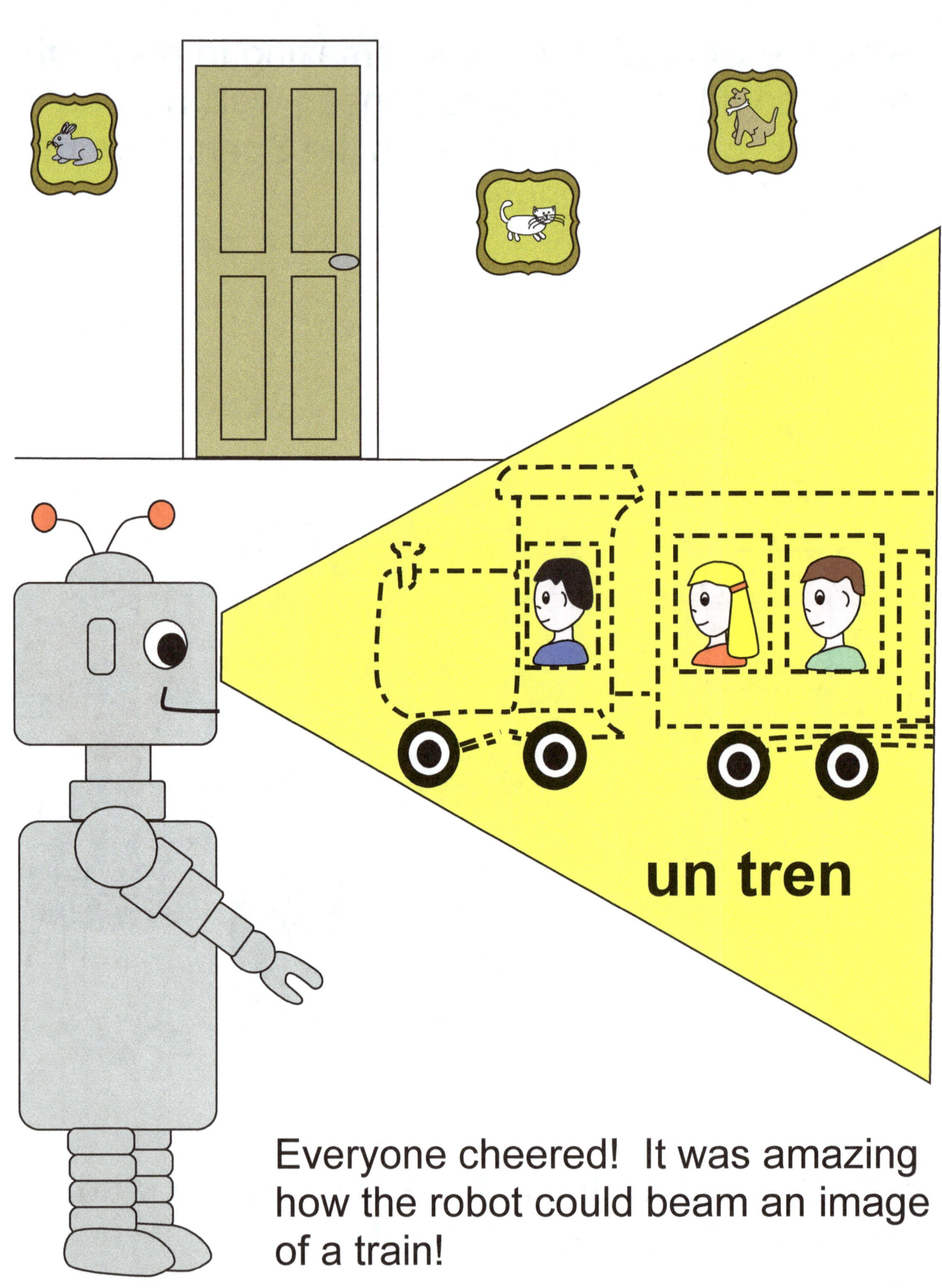

un tren

Everyone cheered! It was amazing how the robot could beam an image of a train!

Daniel and his friends then chose another type of transport.

Everyone moved their chairs into position, and the robot beamed an image of…..

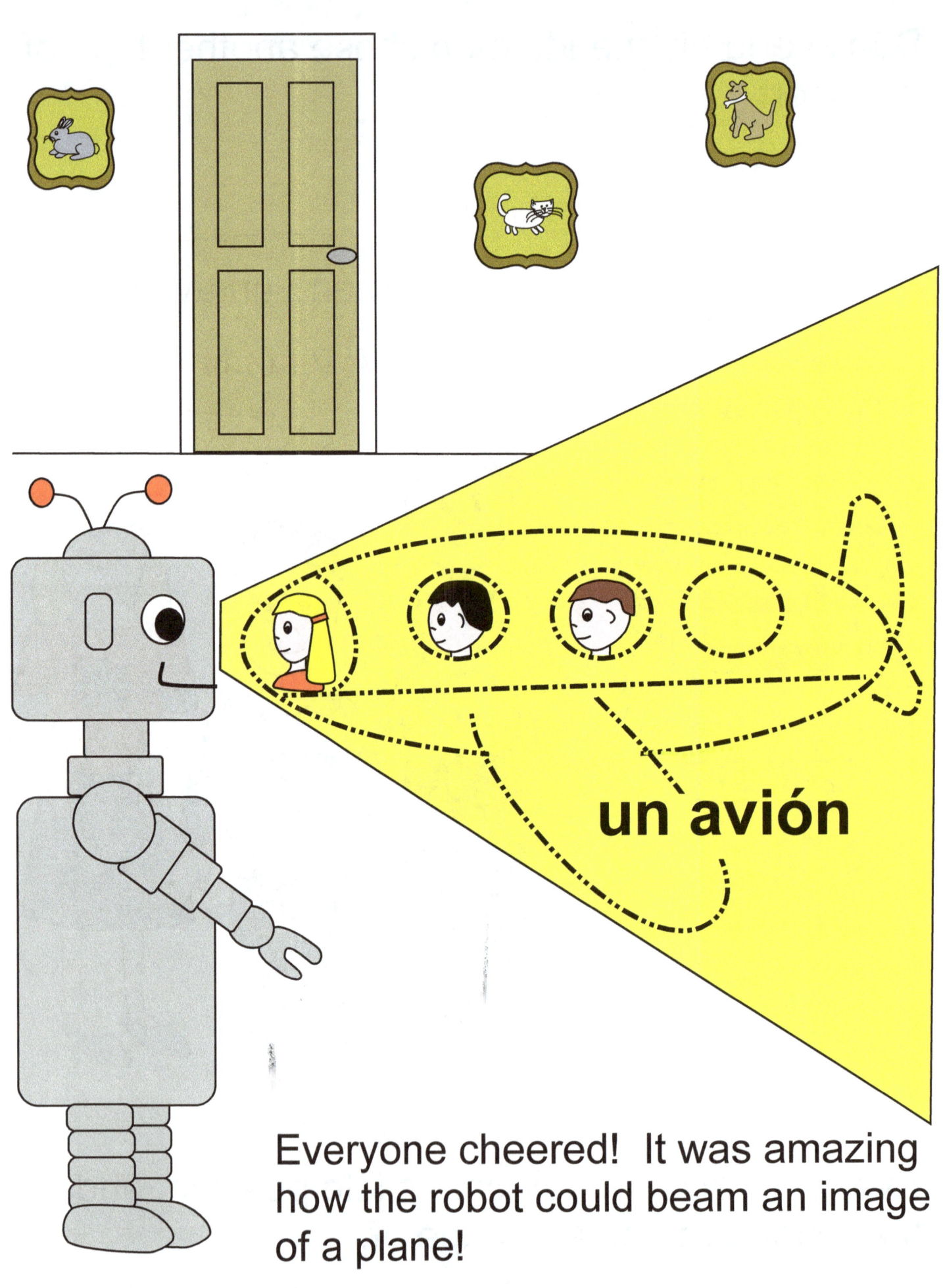

un avión

Everyone cheered! It was amazing how the robot could beam an image of a plane!

Daniel and his friends then chose another type of transport.

Everyone moved their chairs into position, and the robot beamed an image of…..

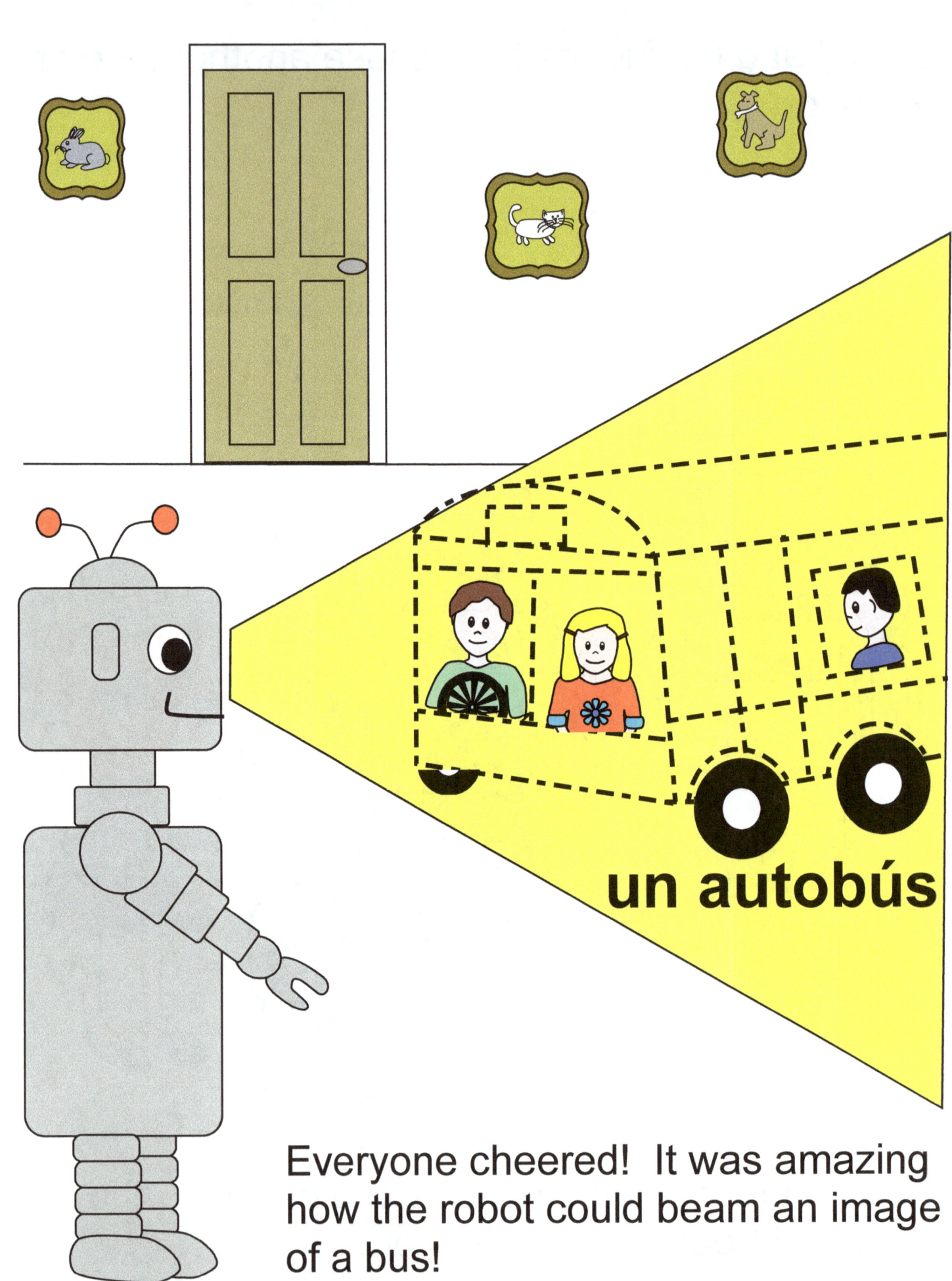

un autobús

Everyone cheered! It was amazing how the robot could beam an image of a bus!

It was getting late, so Daniel and his friends chose one last type of transport..

Un coche   un coche   UN COCHE

Everyone moved their chairs into position, and the robot beamed an image of…..

It had been a fun afternoon!

Can you remember all the Spanish words for the different types of transport?

Lets say them together!

un avión

un autobús

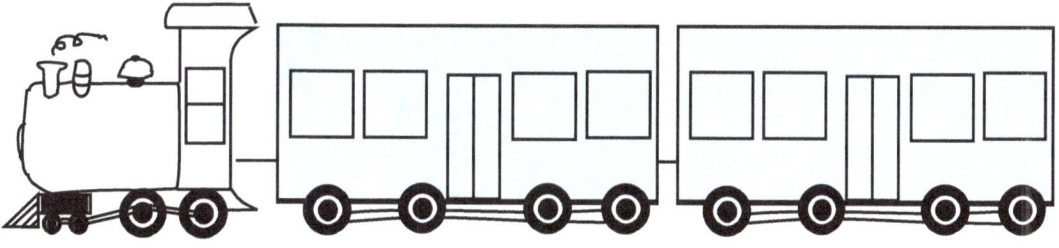

un tren

un coche

It was time to say goodbye, so they all said goodbye in Spanish:

Daniel And the Spanish Robot
The Day Daniel Wasn't Well

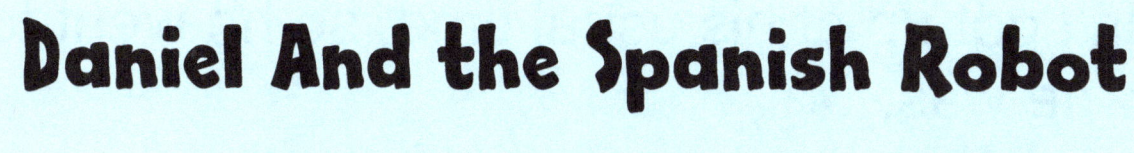

One day, the Spanish robot noticed that Daniel hadn't got up at his usual time, so he went to see how he was:

¿Cómo estás?

Now Daniel wasn't feeling very well, so he replied:

Mal.

Daniel was only feeling a little hungry, so he asked the robot for some biscuits:

"Poor Daniel" thought the robot. "He doesn't really mean biscuits. He's getting his Spanish all muddled up."

So the Spanish robot went away and got….

Unos cereales

Daniel thanked the robot for the cereal, even though he would have preferred some biscuits!

Gracias.

Two hours later the robot went to see Daniel.

"¡Unas galletas! That's not right!" thought the robot. "He will never get better eating biscuits!"

So he went away and brought Daniel........

unas fresas

Daniel thanked the robot for the strawberries. He had asked for biscuits, but he liked strawberries too. And it's good to eat fruit when you are ill.

Gracias.

Daniel's mum came to see how he was.

She liked hearing him speak Spanish, so maybe she would get him some delicious biscuits.

Now his mum also thought that Daniel needed some fruit to help him get better, so she went away and brought him….

It was soon lunchtime, so the robot went to see if his best friend had any requests.

Unas galletas, por favor.

Surely this time the robot would bring him some biscuits! But hearing again "Unas galletas, por favor." the robot decided that Daniel must be very ill as that's all he was repeating!

So he went away and got …..

una sopa

The robot came back and checked that Daniel had eaten all of the **sopa**:

The robot checked the bowl was empty.
He then produced…..

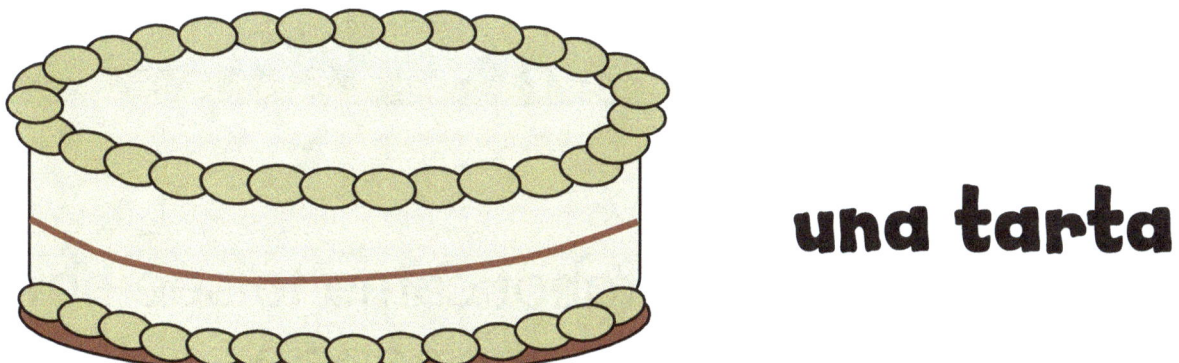

una tarta

Una tarta. Wow! Daniel loved cakes!

He didn't realise they had a delicious cake at home!

The robot cut him a piece, so Daniel thanked him in Spanish. "Gracias."

But Daniel still felt like eating some biscuits!

So he drew a picture of **unas galletas**.

Mid afternoon when the robot came to see how his best friend was, Daniel once again said: "**Unas galletas, por favor**".

This time, Daniel showed the robot the picture of the biscuits he had drawn. "Oh no", thought the Robot. "He really *does* want biscuits!" So he went away and brought……

unas galletas

Daniel was so happy that he finally had some biscuits.

So he said "Thank you! Thank you very much" in Spanish.

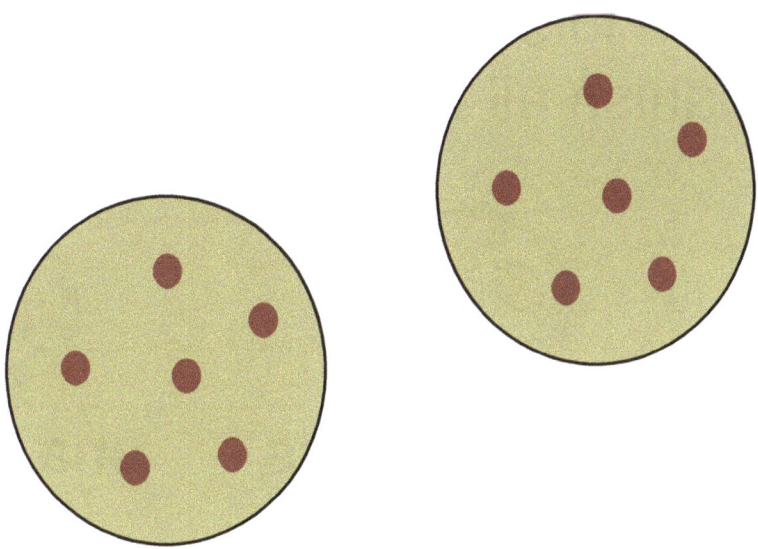

Gracias.

Muchas gracias.

Daniel had eaten lots of nice things. Let's say together in Spanish all the things he's eaten:

unos cereales **unas fresas** **una naranja**

  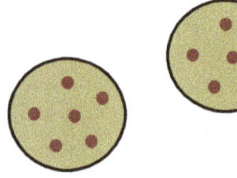

una sopa **una tarta** **unas galletas**

After eating **unas galletas**, Daniel felt a lot better. So he got up! But he knew it was probably

unas fresas , **una naranja** and **una sopa** that had helped him get better, not **unas galletas!**

The Spanish robot was glad to see that Daniel was better. He didn't like seeing his best friend ill.

© **Joanne Leyland**   first edition 2017   second edition 2018   third edition 2021
No part of the story may be photocopied or reproduced digitally without the prior written agreement of the author. The word list and the song lyrics may be photocopied for class or home use by the purchasing institution or individual.

Spanish - English word list

Hola	Hello
Adiós	Goodbye
Sí	Yes
No	No
Por favor	Please
Gracias	Thank you
Muchas gracias	Thank you very much
¿Has acabado?	Have you finished?
¿Cómo estás?	How are you? (to one friend)
¿Cómo estáis?	How are you? (to more than one friend)
Muy bien	I'm very good
Mal	I'm not feeling that good
Me llamo	My name is

1	uno	(one)
2	dos	(two)
3	tres	(three)

Transport

un tren
a train

un avión
an aeroplane

un autobús
a bus

un coche
a car

Food

unos cereales
cereal

unas fresas
some strawberries

una sopa
a soup

una tarta
a cake

una naranja
an orange

unas galletas
some biscuits

© Joanne Leyland - This page may be photocopied by the purchasing individual or institution for use in class or at home

Let's sing a song!

The following words could either be sung to a made up tune, or you could try saying the words as a rap.

For inspiration of a melody to use you could hum first a nursery rhyme. How many different versions can you create using the lyrics?

   unas fresas, unas fresas

   una naranja, una naranja

   una tarta, una tarta

   unas galletas, unas galletas

Follow on activity: Can you remember what order Daniel ate the following things? Look back in the story to see if you remember the correct order!

una sopa

una tarta

unas fresas

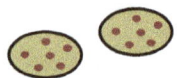
unas galletas

unos cereales

una naranja

© Joanne Leyland - This page may be photocopied by the purchasing individual or institution for use in class or at home

www.ingramcontent.com/pod-product-compliance
Lightning Source LLC
Chambersburg PA
CBHW081359080526
44588CB00016B/2547